Meditations on the Third Chinese Patriarch of Zen's "Verses on the Faith Mind"

Frank White

Meditations on the Third Chinese Patriarch of Zen's "Verses on the Faith Mind"
Copyright © 2023 by Frank White

Published by Multiverse Media Inc. All rights reserved. No part of this book may be reproduced or transmitted in any form or by any means, electronic or mechanical, including photocopying, recording, or by any information storage and retrieval system, without permission in writing from the Publisher.

First printed edition published in 2022 by Multiverse Publishing, LLC.

Print ISBN-13 978-1-960119-86-5
eBook ISBN-13 978-1-960119-85-8

We gratefully acknowledge permission from White Pine Press,
P.O. Box 236, Buffalo, NY 1420, to use excerpts from their book,
The Hsin-Hsin Ming, Verses on the Faith-Mind by Seng-ts'an.
www.whitepine.org

Printed in the United States of America

MULTIVERSE
PUBLISHING
multiversepublishingllc.com

Dedicated to Zen Sensei Josh Dainin White

Meditations on the Third Chinese Patriarch of Zen's "Verses on the Faith Mind"

Preface

From 1966 to 1969, I was a graduate student at Oxford University. It was a turbulent time, not unlike today, and while I was there, I wrote the novel you are about to read.

The manuscript lay dormant for some 40 years, until I published it on Kindle in 2010.

I updated the details to some extent at that time, but the basic story remained the same. That was a decade ago, and much has happened to make *Revolution* seem prescient. When Dylan Taylor, owner of Multiverse Media, acquired the rights to the book, we discussed whether I should revise it more extensively to make it about America in 2020. Ultimately, we decided it might be more interesting for readers to see the book as a kind of historical fiction, or what might have taken place in an alternative future if the 1960s had turned out slightly differently.

I believe the basic message of the book remains valid and perhaps instructive for our time: see what you think as you follow the adventures of the Barrah Gang, the Guevaras, the Panthers, and the Free Children.

Frank White, October 2020

The Great Way* is not difficult for those who have no preferences. When love and hate are both absent, everything becomes clear and undisguised. Make the smallest distinction, however, and heaven and earth are set infinitely apart. If you wish to see the truth, then hold no opinions for, or against, anything. To set up what you like against what you dislike is the disease of the mind. When the deep meaning of things is not understood, the mind's essential peace is disturbed to no avail.

This poem by Seng Ts'an, the third Chinese patriarch of Zen Buddhism, begins, appropriately, with "the Great Way." This Great Way is the same as the Tao, which in itself is not translatable into language. Perhaps most simply, it is "all and everything." All of us are part of the Great Way, and we are journeying on the Great Way.

Note that the patriarch does not say, "The Great Way is easy…" but that it is "not difficult…" for those "who have no preferences."

This is a nuanced distinction, but one that matters. He is saying, I believe, "It is doable, you can make it on this journey." The latter part of the sentence is remarkably deceptive until you read it carefully. For whom is the Great Way not difficult? Those who have no preferences.

This is a simple statement, but it seems to set the bar very high. After all, who is there on this Earth who does not have *preferences*? Since everyone has them, it must mean that the Great Way is actually difficult for all of us. Then, he goes on to say that the absence of love and hate reveals a world that is "clear and undisguised." Our society has reached the point where it is, in theory, ready to do away with all forms of hate (though we haven't achieved it yet). However, what about love? Isn't that the essence of what it means to be a good person, i.e., loving others? In modern parlance, the patriarch seems to be "doubling down." Not only are we urged to have no preferences but we are also told to avoid *both* love and hate. Perhaps the patriarch would say that love is a fine emotion to have, and much better than hate, but it obscures the reality he is trying to reveal, which is a reality that is "clear and undisguised."

Most of us have been "in love" at one time or another, and we know that it can blind us to, for example, imperfections in the beloved. There was even a Rolling Stones song years ago called "Blinded by Love." (I still enjoy listening to it!)

Christians, in particular, may find this perspective difficult to countenance. In Christianity, we are enjoined to love the Lord our God "with all our hearts and all our souls, and our neighbors as ourselves." Love appears to be at the very center of our worship, including our understanding that "God so loved the world that he gave his only begotten son, that whosoever believed in him might not perish, but have everlasting life."

So, from the Christian point of view, it would be hard to let go of our love and still have anything resembling the religion that we practice today. I don't think the patriarch would mind that, though. Zen is not an evangelizing religion, so I believe he would happily allow Christians to have their own beliefs, and simply say, "I am showing you the path to enlightenment."

In that sense, we might make a distinction between salvation and enlightenment. Christianity, through love, shows us how

Meditations on the Third Chinese Patriarch of Zen

to save our souls, while Buddhism, through its transcendence of love and hate, shows us how to be enlightened. Even more to the point, it is not clear that Zen Buddhists believe in a soul, or anything lasting.

I have always found it fascinating that Christians were initially known as "People of the Way," which would seem to place them in the Buddhist tradition. There are also rumors that Jesus traveled to India and studied Buddhism. In the Gospels, Jesus even tells his disciples, "I am the Way…"

Although Buddhism and Christianity seem to be very different, the Way connects the two. Part of the problem may well be that the Christianity we know today is not the whole story. In fact, "orthodox Christians" in the early years after Jesus' death, suppressed many other forms of Christianity, including a particularly strong branch, called Gnosticism. The Gnostics claimed to be disciples of Jesus, but their interpretation of his teachings clashed with orthodoxy, and many "Gnostic gospels" were banned in favor of the four we know today.

In 1945, however, near an Egyptian town called Nag Hammadi, a treasure trove of Gnostic writings, hidden in a cave, came to light. These have kindled a new level of interest in these early "heretics," and their worldviews.

Elaine Pagels, a leading authority on Gnostic thought, points out that one of the documents that came out of that cave, the Gospel of Thomas, could as easily be referring to the Buddha as to Jesus. She notes that it speaks of illusion and enlightenment, not of sin and repentance[1], and she also points out reports that Thomas and his colleagues traveled to India after the death of Jesus.[2] While the physical connections between these two streams of thought are fascinating, they are not so

3

Frank White

important as the clear parallels that exist in the mental realm. So it is possible that Christianity and Buddhism, when both are seen in the broadest possible context, have more in common than we normally believe.

In any event, the patriarch tells us that if we make the "smallest distinction," it will create an infinite gap between heaven and earth. This is a hard lesson to absorb. Of course, all of us make distinctions between good and bad, right and wrong, beautiful and ugly. Isn't it human to do so, and sometimes isn't it necessary to our survival? For example, knowing whether a situation is dangerous or not could save one's life.

The patriarch persists, however, because (I think) in spite of all these rational responses to what he is saying, he wants us to see the seamless interconnections of life, not the differences that divide everything up according to how our limited brains see the world. After all, it is not something inherent in the objects we perceive that is beautiful or ugly, but something in our minds that triggers the response "beautiful" or "ugly."

Often, this is cultural and therefore extremely contingent. For example, western societies have come to adore the hourglass figure in women and to call that beautiful or "sexy." However, there are other cultures where being heavy is considered attractive. Westerners would call it "obese," but members of these other societies would call it "lovely."

I think we have to give this round to Seng Ts'an. Even the most cursory examination of distinctions reveals the extent to which they are transient and illusory. Of course, our brains are wired to see differences, so we are likely to continue doing so, but at least we can know that we are "setting heaven and earth infinitely apart!"

Meditations on the Third Chinese Patriarch of Zen

In the next sentence, we are offered a choice: the opportunity is to "see the truth," and who wouldn't want that? Don't all of us want to see what is true and abandon what is false? Well, if so, says the patriarch, you need to stop holding opinions!

How difficult this would be, of course. All of us have opinions—about politics, economics, culture, music, and sports. And these opinions are often in conflict with one another, which can be stimulating, or a cause of great conflict and consternation. Think about it, though. Do you really believe that your opinion about the Democrats, the Republicans, rap music, or "Game of Thrones" has a universal grounding? You like the Democrats, your brother likes the Republicans, you hate rap, your kids love it, you find "Game of Thrones" weird and violent, your students think it is profound. Who is right and who is wrong?

Christians can find echoes of our faith in the admonition against holding opinions. Jesus said, "Judge not, so that you will not be judged." We have usually taken this to mean that we should not judge others, because our sins are just as great as theirs. However, the idea of judging can be expanded to encompass what the patriarch is saying. Later in the poem, he also talks about "the burdensome practice of judging."

It may seem impossible to give up opinions, but just imagine how liberating it would be—consider it just for a moment.

I once had the experience myself of going to meet someone in a hotel lobby, and arriving early. So I had nothing to do but sit there and watch people go by. I noticed at first that I was very judgmental, making up stories about the individuals and who they were, ranking them as handsome and attractive, or plain and unattractive. Then, slowly but surely, as I continued to watch, I stopped judging and simply saw the ebb and flow of very different looking people, each one going about their business and living their lives. I began to see all of them together as part of the whole that we call humanity, and each of them was unique and special.

This is a revelation and a revolution in thought that is difficult to achieve, and I only had the experience by accident. Nor does it necessarily last. Not long afterward, I was back to judging and holding opinions!

The patriarch doesn't kid around about this topic, though. He doesn't say that making distinctions is sort of a bad thing we ought to avoid. He goes beyond that and says it is a "disease," a disease of the mind.

He is telling us that, counterintuitively, everything we believe makes for a healthy mind is actually a sickness! If you have ever experienced a chronic disease, you know how disheartening it can be to know that something is wrong with your body and it is not going away any time soon. Perhaps, even closer to what the patriarch is talking about, you may have had a mental illness, say obsessive compulsive disorder. It is getting in the way of your life, and you don't like it, but you can't fix it alone. You need the help of a trained professional, perhaps a psychiatrist, psychologist, or therapist to get yourself back to normal.

Thus, Seng Ts'an is telling us that we are mentally ill, and that the cure is simple: stop doing what we are doing. He is functioning like the doctor, psychologist, or therapist who has made a diagnosis and is now prescribing medicine for it—and tough medicine it is, indeed!

Again, we see echoes of this mentality in Christianity. Jesus enjoins us to love our enemies and do good to those who hate us. Otherwise, aren't we just like the nonbelievers who make a clear distinction between friends and foes? Jesus also points out that God allows the sun to shine on and the rain to fall on the just and the unjust, the righteous and unrighteous alike. Later in Romans, Paul tells Christians not to seek revenge on enemies because "Vengeance is mine," saith the Lord.

We don't know, from these passages about setting up what we like against what we dislike, if the disease is acute and curable, chronic and manageable, or terminal and hopeless. However, perhaps we can assume it is not terminal and hopeless, or the patriarch would not be writing about it. What would be the point, if there is nothing to be done?

As for the other two options, the treatment is pretty much the same, isn't it? We need to find ways to stop setting up what we like and what we dislike. Isn't this a bit like saying, "Don't think of pink elephants?" Immediately, unbidden by you, the image of a pink elephant appears in your mind.

This is, of course, the great challenge of Zen, i.e., doing by not doing. You will find liberation by ceasing to set up what you like against what you dislike, but as soon as you try to do that, you will fail. As more modern philosophers have said, "Trying is lying." So you can't try to stop, you have to just stop.

This is also why Zen puts so much emphasis on meditation, rather than talking about philosophy or theology. If you spend enough time just watching your breath, you may eventually reach a state of enlightenment, which you will not reach by talking about enlightenment.

The patriarch concludes this verse by letting us know that disease is not the natural state of our minds. The mind, he says, is essentially peaceful, and that is the state to be attained.

It is attained, not by trying, but by letting go of judgments and distinctions. If we are to try anything, it is to understand "the deep meaning of things." What is this deep meaning? That all is one.

When we don't see this reality, the mind's peace is disturbed, "to no avail." In other words, it creates suffering, and provides nothing of value.

Our brains fool us into an illusion of separateness and lack of connection. There is me, there is you, there are other people, animals, plants, and so on, and we need to make judgments about them in order to survive, to perpetuate our individual existence.

This is, however, only one perspective.

When astronauts leave the Earth and look back at our planet, all the chaos and diversity seen on the surface disappears, and they see a beautiful, awe-inspiring oneness, a single, interconnected system. This is a cognitive shift I have named "the Overview Effect."[3]

Our goal, then, is to grasp this deep meaning of oneness, and when we do, the mind will be peaceful.

The Way is perfect, like vast space where nothing is lacking and nothing is in excess. Indeed, it is due to our choosing to accept or reject that we do not see the true nature of things. Live neither in the entanglements of outer things, nor in inner feelings of emptiness. Be serene in the oneness of things, and such erroneous views will disappear by themselves. When you try to stop activity to achieve passivity, your very effort fills you with activity. As long as you remain in one extreme or the other, you will never know Oneness.

In this verse, the patriarch returns to the theme of his first verse, i.e., the Way. He states that it is "perfect." Once again, he challenges our limited notions of what is possible. We tend to think that nothing is perfect in this world of ours, or even in this universe in which we live.

Again, as a comparison with Christianity, we do think of God as perfect, and of Jesus as being the perfect human, without sin. So we have some concept of perfection, but we consider it to be extremely rare. Jesus called himself, the Way, the truth, and the life, so perhaps God and the Way are the same?

Regardless, the Way is compared with "vast space, where nothing is lacking and nothing is in excess." The Way is the whole system of which we are a part, and that is, in my opinion, what all spiritual practices point to, wholeness, or "that which is holy."

In a refrain that is growing familiar, the patriarch reminds us that it is our decision to accept or reject that hides the true nature of reality from our eyes. We live in a perfect environment, but we choose not to see it. The use of the word "choosing" is critical to this passage. If we had no choice in the matter, all would be lost, wouldn't it? We would simply be condemned to a state of ignorance, restlessly accepting and rejecting, longing for a state we could never attain.

However, we *do* have a choice to stop accepting and rejecting, and then we will view reality as it actually is. The truth is that our entire life is made up of choices, isn't it? How we treat our parents, whom we choose to marry (or not to marry), what profession to take up, and whether to have a religious practice or not, and on and on. Even if we find our lives to be something other than we think we wanted, we have to accept that we created those lives by our day-to-day choices. In true

Buddhist fashion, the patriarch does not recommend an extreme response to his message. He suggests the "Middle Way" of the Buddha, exhorting the readers of this poem to avoid becoming entangled in the outer world, but also to beware on the solipsism of focusing too heavily on the inner life, a pitfall for many spiritual people.

If there is any one passage that sums of his message, it is the one following this warning, which is to: "be serene in the oneness of things." If the Way is perfect, with nothing lacking and nothing in excess, then why be worried about anything that happens within that context? If we are able to focus our attention, instead, on the oneness of things, we will achieve serenity.

Once again, though we may not be looking for it, we find striking parallels with Christianity, and Jesus' advice for his "People of the Way." In the Gospel of Matthew, he enjoins his followers not to worry about daily frustrations in life.

Therefore I tell you, do not worry about your life, what you will eat or drink; or about your body, what you will wear. Is not life more than food, and the body more than clothes? Look at the birds of the air; they do not sow or reap or store away in barns, and yet your heavenly Father feeds them. Are you not much more valuable than they? Can any one of you by worrying add a single hour to your life?

So do not worry, saying, 'What shall we eat?' or 'What shall we drink?' or 'What shall we wear?' For the pagans run after all these things, and your heavenly Father knows that you need them. But seek first his kingdom and his righteousness, and all these things will be given to you as well. Therefore, do not worry about tomorrow, for tomorrow will worry about itself. Each day has enough trouble of its own."[4] It's a bit sad that

Meditations on the Third Chinese Patriarch of Zen

we modern humans have more comfort and possessions and good health than even kings and queens did in the time of Jesus. Yet, we are often "stressed out" and have to take pills to keep from having "panic attacks" over the daily frustrations of our lives. We *do* worry about tomorrow, even though, as Jesus says, it won't help us at all. In this, Jesus and Seng Ts'an are in accord.

Here, we see another parallel between the teachings of Jesus and those of the patriarch. Jesus says that we should seek God's kingdom and his righteousness and everything will fall into place. Seng Ts'an says that we don't need to fight against "erroneous views." If we are serene in the oneness of things, these mistaken perceptions will disappear of their own accord.

You might think that in order to achieve this serenity, we need to go off and meditate day and night. However, that is not the Way. The patriarch points out that trying to stop activity to achieve some kind of passive acceptance just fills you with activity in and of itself. Zen is famous for having little patience with "trying," and this is no exception.

The patriarch finishes this verse by warning against any kind of extreme approach to enlightenment because any extreme position takes you away from the goal of Oneness. We really need to hear this warning, because many spiritual or religious people go to extremes to reach a higher plane of existence. I am reminded of the Zen prescription for a happy life: "When tired, sleep, when hungry, eat." As the great Zen masters would say, "Nothing special!"

Imagine a dialogue between Seng Ts'an and Jesus about this topic. Do you think they would be in agreement or in conflict with one another? I think they would agree wholeheartedly.

Frank White

Those who do not live in the single Way fail in both activity and passivity, assertion and denial. To deny the reality of things is to miss their reality; to assert the emptiness of things is to miss their reality. The more you talk and think about it, the further astray you wander from the truth. Stop talking and thinking, and there is nothing you will not be able to know.

In this verse, the patriarch begins to describe what it is like for those who live outside of the Way, which is, of course, most of us! He gives us the image of these people bouncing back and forth between being very active and being very passive, in asserting that the material world is important and claiming that it is meaningless.

The distinction reminds me of the practical, pragmatic, and materialistic person who takes nothing on faith, and is convinced only by empirical evidence, and the existentialist, who believes that nothing is meaningful outside the meaning we ourselves give it.

In a clear warning to the intellectuals among us, the patriarch lets us know that talking about this topic, and even thinking about it, will get in the way of direct perception of truth. Once again, this is a challenging perspective, but a very Zen point of view. Zen speaks to a direct apprehension of a truth that is beyond words, so talking and thinking are obviously not the way to get there.

The patriarch tells us that if we stop talking and thinking, we will be able to know everything, or put another way, there is "nothing we will not be able to know." This way of knowing is different from that which the academics profess. It is a state of consciousness that we might call enlightenment.

We have a choice, then, which is to focus on words, debates, discussions, and so-called knowledge, or we can simply let go of all that and *experience* "the truth."

To return to the root is to find the meaning, but to pursue appearances is to miss the source. At the moment of inner enlightenment, there is going beyond appearance and emptiness. The changes that appear to occur in the empty world we call real only because of our ignorance. Do not search for the truth; only cease to cherish opinions.

What does it mean "to return to the root?" I think it implies that there is some absolute reality that stands behind all the "appearances" that float before us in the world of senses and ideas. The patriarch has it right, that we "pursue" these appearances, and that is the source of our ongoing discontent. We "miss the source," which is the essential underlying reality of the world around us, that from which everything else springs.

When we connect with that source, we will have a moment of inner enlightenment. The back-and-forth of appearance and emptiness fades away, and we are one with the universe. We leave behind the constant to-and-fro of changes in the world, which are illusory, against the background of oneness.

The patriarch concludes this verse with an admonition similar to the way in which he ended the previous section, where he suggests that we stop trying to find all the answers, and simply "stop talking and thinking," and we will know everything. Here, he tells us to stop searching for the truth and simply (again) "cease" all the "doing," in this case cherishing our opinions.

Once again, we see the Zen way of "achieving through not achieving." Rather than trying to accomplish something, we are urged just to let go of the things that are in the way of accomplishment. It is a very difficult lesson for the Western mind!

Can you imagine not having an opinion about everything around you? Consider not having an opinion about Donald Trump, Bernie Sanders, Hillary Clinton, and Ted Cruz. Consider not having an opinion about Islam, Christianity, and Judaism. Consider not having an opinion about Sedona, Boston, and Paris. It's not easy to do, is it?

I can say from personal experience that it is possible, though. I have had fleeting moments of what the Buddhists call *kensho*, or enlightenment, when all is one and there is "neither coming nor going."

It happened recently as I took a mundane walk on a nearby street in my neighborhood. There was nothing special about the moment or the setting. I was looking at the same houses, trees, lawns, and animals that I saw every day on that path. But suddenly, I stopped and for just a moment, really SAW all of it without the constant interruptions of one thought after another intruding. Nothing had changed on Winnemay Street; what had shifted was my perception and my thought processes.

As the patriarch said in an earlier verse, "Stop talking and thinking, and there is nothing you will not be able to know." At that moment, I was walking, not talking, and for a split second, I stopped thinking. It's critical in this instance to understand what the patriarch means by "know." He is pointing to a form of knowing that is Buddhist in nature, a knowing by direct perception rather than through words and concepts. Here, it

Meditations on the Third Chinese Patriarch of Zen

is similar to a suppressed branch of Christianity, called Gnosticism, which, as Elaine Pagels and other writers have put it, makes Jesus sound more like the Buddha than like an orthodox Christian[5].

In any event, even though that moment (and others like it) represented only an infinitesimal portion of my entire life, I know from having experienced it that Seng Ts'an is pointing to something real, something attainable. Of course, having heard how great this *kensho* thing is, you might ask, "How can I get it?" Any Zen master, including Seng T'san would likely answer, "Meditate!"

Zen meditation is nothing more and nothing less than sitting quietly and watching your breath. While you are doing that, all kinds of thoughts will come rolling through your mind. The whole point is to, as the est training (a close cousin of Zen) says, "Thank your mind for sharing and move on." Meditation is not really the topic of this treatise, but I mention it because it would be wrong to think that the patriarch is telling the reader to aspire to something that cannot be attained.

In fact, Zen meditation, and Zen itself, represents a technology designed to achieve precisely what Seng T'san is highlighting here.

Do not remain in the dualistic state; avoid such pursuits carefully. If there is even a trace of this and that, of right and wrong, the Mind-essence will be lost in confusion. Although all dualities come from the One, do not be attached even to this One. When the mind exists undisturbed in the Way, nothing in the world can offend, and when a thing can no longer offend, it ceases to exist in the old way.

Clearly, the opposite of Oneness is dualism, and the dynamic between the two is obvious throughout human history and the life of the mind. In fact, the apparent conflict between Oneness and Duality runs the risk of becoming a duality all on its own.

This is why the patriarch tells us to get out of the dualistic state, no matter what. And it needs to be a complete escape from duality, not a partial one. He even warns us about getting too focused on oneness itself, because that can become an anxiety-producing attachment as well. Put another way, we would be turning an experience into a concept if we say, "I am seeking oneness."

From what I have learned about the patriarch's philosophy, I would think that he would suggest we not seek oneness, but rather that *we remove the barriers to experiencing it.*

The patriarch urges us to avoid anything that objectifies reality. Yes, he says, there is the One, but to be focused on the *idea* of the One will prevent you from *experiencing* it.

And he lets us know something pretty amazing; it is a disappearing act. Once you get to a certain stage of enlightenment, nothing can offend you, and when that happens, what used to be offensive disappears. It no longer exists. This is interesting, because I received my copy of this treatise when I took the est training in the late 1970s. One of the things the leaders emphasize in est is "What you resist, persists." So if you really don't like the fact that you are an ambitious asshole, and keep pretending to be a very spiritual person, you will never get beyond being an ambitious asshole. However, if you embrace and acknowledge fully your ambition, that aspect of yourself will disappear.

This represents yet another example of the Zen approach of

"doing by not doing." Don't *try* to be a better person, just embrace the reality that you really are not and see what happens. (Another est principle is "Trying is lying." Don't ever say you will *try* to do something; either do it or don't do it. Interestingly, this is a dictum of Master Yoda in *Star Wars*.)

There is, I think, an interesting example of this kind of thinking in the teachings of Jesus. Jesus tells us to love our enemies and do good to those who hurt us.

This sounds wonderful, but I can tell you from experience that it is hard to do. However, consider this: as long as you hate your enemy, he or she is just that, your enemy. If you continue to resist their humanity and define them as "other," they persist as an enemy and you have a threatening presence in your life, even if only in your mind. Once you do good to your enemy, however, it is difficult to think of them in a negative way any longer, not because of anything they have done, but because of what *you have done* and, in most cases, your anger and hurt will simply disappear.

Jesus went through horrible torture and pain before he died on the cross, but he forgave those who had inflicted this suffering on him before he died. He asked that God would forgive them because of their ignorance: "they know not what they do." If we see our enemies in that same way, we can forgive them, just as we would forgive any mistake made from lack of knowledge.

When no discriminating thoughts arise, the old mind ceases to exist. When thought objects vanish, the thinking-subject vanishes, as when the mind vanishes, objects vanish. Things are objects because of the subject (mind); the mind (subject) is such because of things (objects). Understand the relativity of these two and the basic reality: the unity of emptiness. In this Emptiness the two are indistinguishable and each contains, in itself, the whole world. If you do not discriminate between coarse and fine, you will not be tempted to prejudice and opinion.

Now, we're getting somewhere! If we follow the sage's advice, we will go beyond making incremental improvements to the "old mind." In fact, it will cease to exist!

He is telling us that the dichotomy of subject/object, which dominates our existence, but is an illusion, will go away when the old mind goes away. How do we get the old mind to disappear? Well, it all goes back to the discriminating thoughts that the patriarch has been condemning from the very start.

He notes that when "thought-objects vanish," the thinking subject also vanishes. This begins a discussion of how to move beyond the distinction of self and other.

The patriarch is sharing an incredibly important insight about the nature of identity in these passages. He is showing that we cannot have an identity of self without an understanding of "other." So when we objectify things to create ourselves as subject, that is how our identity arises.

Buddhists consider the idea of a fixed identity to be an illusion, in any case. They note that, from moment to moment, we really are not the same person. Our bodies are changing as cells die and are replaced, and our mental states change as well, moving from one thought to another, fixing on one object after another. More than that, they consider desire to be at the heart of all suffering. The subject desires the objects and, once it attains an object (getting a new house, for example), it is not satisfied, but begins to desire some other object (a new car).

In many ways, this kind of limited consciousness is a "con." We are conned into believing that "having something" will make us happy, rather than "being someone."

The sage sees subject and object as relative. What, then, is absolute? He calls "emptiness" the basic unity. We do not think of emptiness as a good thing, of course. If you look for a definition, you will find the dictionary refers to a state of containing nothing, or "no-thing." However, for Zen Buddhists, emptiness is the pathway to enlightenment.

Zen masters exalt the notion of "don't know mind," a state of being in which one does not pretend to know anything, but rather is open to everything. There is a famous story of a professor who goes to visit a Zen master. He is there supposedly to learn, but it becomes clear that he really just wants to talk about his own ideas. The sage offers him tea and begins pouring, but does not stop when the cup is filled, so it overflows.

His visitor says, "Stop, stop, it is full!"

The master tells him that the cup is like his mind, full of ideas, and he must "empty his mind," before he can learn anything.[6]

Once again, we find a surprising analog to this notion in the teachings of Jesus, found in the Gospel of Matthew, 11:25:

At that time Jesus declared, "I thank thee, Father, Lord of heaven and earth, that thou hast hidden these things from the wise and understanding and revealed them to babes...[7]

Jesus is essentially mirroring the thinking of the Zen master as he poured the tea for the professor. The wonderful thing about babies is that they are open to the world around them. They are always learning and absorbing what they can in an open and often joyous manner. I don't mean to say that children are a blank slate. Any parent will tell you that they can see early signs of a distinct personality even in a newborn.

However, you can also see their openness to learning new knowledge. It is no accident that they constantly ask adults questions, and the query most often posed is, "Why?" They want to know "first causes," as philosophers and theologians would say.

As we grow older, certain patterns develop in our brains and we create a "world view," or way of seeing everything around us. The truth is that, as physical beings, this is a survival mechanism. Our brains begin to develop assumptions about the outside world, based on experience, as simple as "Don't stick your hand in the fire," and "Be sure you have shelter when the sun goes down."

In our complex technological society, it is more like, "Don't tell your boss he is an idiot," and "Pay your bills on time."

In some cases, these filters become barriers to new experiences or relationships. In fact, they can become poisonous if they transmute in racism, homophobia, or xenophobia. Thus, an evolutionary filter that says, "Be wary of people different from you," which might have served a person well in a primitive culture without the rule of law, becomes a stereotype that is detrimental to everyone concerned in a modern society.

At the other end of the spectrum is the state of enlightenment described by the Third Chinese Patriarch. In the Emptiness he pictures for us, the subject and object dichotomy goes away or become indistinguishable.

The patriarch closes this verse with a challenge: "Don't discriminate between coarse and fine." It is, of course, a difficult challenge to meet. Is it possible not to know the difference between sandpaper and silk? Of course, that is impossible, but sandpaper has a role to play in the world, and so does silk. Each is perfect in its own way. You wouldn't use sandpaper to make clothing, and you wouldn't use silk to sand wood into a piece of furniture.

Isn't this the whole point of the discourse? What makes the universe perfect is not that everything is the same and homogeneous, but that there is great diversity in it, and yet it is unified as well—by emptiness.

To live in the great Way is neither easy nor difficult, but those with limited views are fearful and irresolute; the faster they hurry, the slower they go. And clinging (attachment) cannot be limited. Even to be attached to the idea of enlightenment is to go astray. Just let things be in their own way, and there will be neither coming nor going. Obey the nature of things (your own nature) and you will walk freely and undisturbed.

In this verse, the patriarch offers up a kind of coda: he began this poem by noting that the Great Way is "not difficult." Now, he returns to this theme by expanding on it and saying that living in the Way is "neither easy nor difficult." So, we don't really have to be stressed about what it is like to live in this fashion. The problem is with people who cannot see the big picture. They rush around, searching for something they think will make things better. But "the faster they hurry, the slower they go!"

The more we pursue something that exists only in the future, the less we can see right before us, the present, which is really the only moment in which we can live. And, of course, if we have learned anything from this great sage so far, we know that living in the moment, without judgment of it, is the way to enlightenment.

However, even though the goal is enlightenment, the paradox is that we won't get there by being attached to this ultimate destination in our journey. In fact, we won't get there by clinging or being attached to anything. This statement is reminiscent of another Zen saying, "If you meet the Buddha on the road, kill him!"

To the non-Buddhist, this sounds nonsensical. Why would you kill the Buddha? It is a shocking statement, and it is meant to shock.

There are many interpretations of this statement, but I believe it means that you don't want anything to get in your "way" as you travel on the "Way." Even the Buddha, whom you might be tempted to stop and worship in some fashion, needs to be removed from your path.

The patriarch says we should "let things be in their own way." Of course, this makes sense, if the Way is perfect. Why would we try to modify things rather than just letting them be? If we do that, "there will be neither coming nor going." In other words, we will find ourselves in the stillness of enlightenment. This really goes against the grain of the Western mind, which is so caught up in reform and progress and making the world a better place.

However, even the most ardent Western thinker has to admit that, once one problem has been solved, something new crops up, and the cycle is unending. Personally, I am not able to move to the position where I don't think we should strive for social justice or try to right wrongs, but it does put this constant striving in context.

What, then, does the sage mean when he says we should obey the nature of things, which is "our own nature?"

I believe he is saying that we need first to understand reality as it is, before we start imposing out standards on it. Jesus said we should not try to take a speck out of our neighbor's eye before we remove the plank in our own eye. To be a reformer often means ignoring our part in the injustices that exist and projecting evil thoughts and deeds onto others. It makes us feel good, and we can ignore our own shortcomings, which are crowded out by righteous anger.

The patriarch is warning us against falling into this trap, though we might still feel compelled to right wrongs and work for social justice. Is it possible to do so without demonizing others? I think the answer is yes, we can protest when things are going wrong while remembering that the people we are protesting against are human as well.

When thought is in bondage, the truth is hidden, for everything is murky and unclear, and the burdensome practice of judging brings annoyance and weariness. What benefit can be derived from distinctions and separation?

Here, the patriarch returns to the problem of being judgmental. He says that it puts our thoughts into a form of bondage, which hides the truth from us. What is the result of judging? Nothing but "annoyance and weariness." In his view, there is no benefit to be gained from making distinctions and separating from the unity of oneness. Now that you have heard what this wise person has to say about it, what benefits do you see from making distinctions and creating separation? Is it something you have to do, or something your mind automatically does? If you simply observe it happening, I would suggest you will see it as having a kind of automaticity to it.

If you wish to move in the one Way, do not dislike even the world of senses and ideas. Indeed, to accept them fully is identical with true enlightenment. The wise man strives to no goals, but the foolish man fetters himself. There is one Dharma, not many; distinctions arise from the clinging needs of the ignorant. To seek Mind with the (discriminating) mind is the greatest of all mistakes.

This is an incredibly rich verse. It begins with what seems to be a contradiction. After all the admonitions about avoiding distinctions and judgments, the Third Chinese Patriarch seems to ask us to embrace them again. However, it really isn't as paradoxical as it seems. The patriarch is really asking us to embrace everything, from the most metaphysical to the most physical, from the domain of spirit to the domain of thought.

Accepting the world of senses and ideas does not mean acting in accord with them or being attached to them. It means accepting that they exist and hold an important reality in the lives of many people. In fact, fully accepting them is consistent with true enlightenment.

The patriarch goes on to make a startling statement, which is that the wise man "strives to no goals." The western mind again asks, "How can this be the case? Isn't it true that if you have no goals, you will just drift through life, and never accomplish anything?"

Well, the problem with goals is that they focus on the future, which of course never actually arrives! Zen wants us to live in the present, to see fully what is happening in this moment, rather than focusing our gaze on something that is eventually coming into being, but is not yet here. The other problem with the future is that it never quite lives up to our imagination of it, because events intervene and reshape our lives as we move forward from the "now."

Wait, now, you are saying, "Isn't it true that if I set a goal, I can reach it?" Yes, of course. Let's say you want to get a book published, something I longed to do for many years. I worked hard on that goal, and eventually I achieved it. Did it make me happy? Yes, very much. However, I ~~think~~ wanted to have the book make a lot of money (it didn't) and to publish a series of books on the same topic (that didn't happen, either). If you want to achieve things in this world, goal setting is a good idea, because it keeps you moving, always looking for the "next big thing." However, if you want to achieve enlightenment, it clearly gets in the way.

So what did you miss while you were focused on that single goal? What opportunities jumped up in your face and waved at you, saying, "Look at me, look at me!"

I have just read a very interesting article by a writer named Rohit Sharma about predicting the future, and shaping it. He suggests the following:

Emergent flexibility is a key advantage as nothing is cast in stone; strategies are built overnight and are always rapidly evolving.[8]

Interestingly, he wrote this in answer to a question on the Quora website in February 2016 as to the possibility that

Frank White

Donald Trump would become president of the United States. He does not support Trump, but analyzed the Trump campaign using tools he invented, and these frameworks indicate that entrepreneurs or politicians whose strategies emerge naturally do much better than those who are oriented toward planning everything. His point is that the future unfolds in complex ways and there are many alternative futures that one might follow.

So this might be what the sage is getting at when he says that the foolish man "fetters himself."

Then the patriarch returns to the theme of oneness when he points out that there is one Dharma, not many. He also targets the cause of distinctions arising as being the needs of those who are "ignorant." Bear in mind that he does not say "stupid." There is a difference between being ignorant of something and not having the mental capacity to grasp something. Neither "ignorant" nor "stupid" are nice things to say about someone, but the distinction is important.

The patriarch closes this verse with the paradoxical statement that seeking Mind with a big "M" with the discriminating mind with a little "m" is the greatest of all mistakes. Now that we have learned a bit more about how he sees the world, this makes perfect sense, though it seems paradoxical.

Mind with a capital "M" is the ineffable oneness that seems to be the goal of Zen training, the space we reach where we move beyond distinctions and see the whole. This is why academic knowledge, valuable though it may be, is not enough to reach enlightenment. It comes from the mind, and breaks things down into parts, but rarely approaches the whole, which is holy.

Meditations on the Third Chinese Patriarch of Zen

A more direct way of putting it might have been, "To seek Mind with the discriminating *brain* is the greatest of all mistakes."

The brain is a marvelous tool, but it does not hold all the secrets of the universe, powerful though it may be. So, while we may allow it to discriminate as a survival mechanism, and even as an engine of evolution, we must not confuse it with the transcendent Mind.

Rest and unrest derive from illusion; with enlightenment there is no liking and disliking. All dualities come from ignorant inference. They are like dreams or flowers in air; foolish to try to grasp them. Gain and loss, right and wrong; such thoughts must finally be abolished at once.

The ultimate goal of Zen Buddhism is, of course, enlightenment. It is a direct comprehension of reality, an experience that is beyond what the ordinary brain/mind can attain. Zen practitioners spend very little time studying texts and spinning out new ideas about the nature of things. Instead, they focus on meditation, physical work, and the effort to grasp the meaning of koans. These are sayings like "What is the sound of one hand clapping?" that baffle the logical mind, but help the seeker of wisdom to break through to what the sage calls "Mind."

In this verse, the patriarch repeats themes that have already been developed earlier in the poem. He asserts that there are no real dualities, and he also reiterates that false understandings come from ignorance. This is one of the areas where Gnostic Christianity and Buddhism overlap. The Gnostics actually got their name from their adversaries within the church, who accused them of seeking secret knowledge (gnosis) not available to everyone.

Frank White

Whether this is true or not, there were Christians who advocated seeking self-knowledge, and elevated that quality above holding onto a set of immutable beliefs. In this way, again, the Gnostics demonstrate a close connection to Zen and to Buddhism in general. In the Gnostic Gospel of Thomas, we are told that the Kingdom of Heaven is "within." This is precisely what the Third Chinese Patriarch is telling us.

If the eye never sleeps, all dreams will naturally cease. If the mind makes no discriminations, the ten thousand things are as they are, of single essence. To understand the mystery of this One-essence is to be released from all entanglements. When all things are seen equally, the timeless Self-essence is reached. No comparisons or analogies are possible in this causeless, relationless state.

The sage states the obvious here: if it were physically possible to avoid sleep, then we would not dream. In the same way, he is telling us that we do not have to strain to realize that everything is of a single essence; all we have to do is stop discriminating among things. In the next two sentences, he links "One-essence" with the timeless "Self-essence." Since discovering the true self is the equivalent of enlightenment, then discovering this One-essence is also the same as being enlightened.

When we are able to grasp this Oneness, the Self-essence, which is outside of time, is attained. At this point, we move beyond causes and relationships to something else altogether. It must be obvious by now that, while the patriarch is using words to point to enlightenment, that state is an experience that transcends words. As he says, comparisons and analogies are no longer relevant.

Consider movement stationary, and the stationary in motion;

both movement and rest disappear. When such dualities cease to exist, Oneness itself cannot exist. To this ultimate finality no law or description applies.

As we approach the end of the discourse, the patriarch reminds us that even Oneness is a concept, a *word* that points to something unspoken and inconceivable. It seems that what we have been seeking all along here is this kind of unity, but when we get to it, even that dissolves into non-existence.

When being in motion and being stationary are interchangeable, all is one, but even then, it must be experienced, and it cannot be an intellectual construct; it is an "ultimate finality." It cannot be bound by laws and it cannot even be fully described.

For the unified mind in accord with the Way, all self-centered striving ceases. Doubts and irresolutions vanish, and life in true faith is possible. With a single stroke we are freed from bondage; nothing clings to us and we hold to nothing. All is empty, clear, self-illuminating, with no exertion of the mind's power. Here thought, feeling, knowledge and imagination are of no value. In this world of Suchness, there is neither self nor other-than-self.

In commenting on this very rich verse, I must digress and become a bit personal. On a recent reading of this passage, I had a brief experience of kensho, as the Zen Buddhists say. I understand kensho to be a kind of flash of enlightenment that comes and goes, and is not permanent. However, it is something one never forgets.

My experience centered on the first sentence: "For the unified mind in accord with the Way, all self-centered striving ceases." As a person who has been driven by self-centered striving all my life, this hit me with great force, and for a moment, I felt how wonderful that state would be. I could see, with great clarity, how much suffering my own "self-centered striving" had caused me all of my life.

I also responded to the phrase, "With a single stroke, we are freed from bondage." Although it seemed impossible after my years of trying to become free of such striving, I understood intuitively that it did happen in a moment. I also "got it" that if I let go of all the things I was holding onto with my ego, nothing would be holding me back or holding me down.

In a kind of crescendo of denial of worldly things, the patriarch tells us that in this place of being, thought, feeling, knowledge, and imagination no longer have any value. That about covers everything, doesn't it?

The key to this whole passage appears at the end, when the sage asserts that, once you reach this state, there is neither self, nor other than self. In other words, your limited and limiting identity has disappeared and you are one with the universe. This really is the aim of Zen, and of Buddhism in general, i.e., the realization that our notion of Self is false.

Do we know what Suchness is, though? We should not rush over this unfamiliar word to plunge into the conversation about the false self. "Suchness" is not easily defined, as is the case with many Zen words and ideas. Also described as "thatness," it is the "direct experience of things as they really are." Michael Molloy says:

We know we are experiencing the "thatness" of reality when we experience something and say to ourselves, "Yes, that's it; that is the way things are." In the moment, we recognize that reality is wondrously beautiful but also that its patterns are fragile and passing.[9]

In Zen, the meaning of "Suchness" or "thatness" is much greater than it at first seems. It really is *everything*, the all-in-all, but more than that, it is the direct perception of reality as it is, rather than as we see it through false perceptions or concepts.

In est, a Western approach to self-realization that borrows heavily from Zen (and where I first came into contact with the Verses on the Faith-Mind by being given a small booklet containing the poem), this notion is communicated by talking about "getting it" or statements like "What is is, and what isn't isn't."

So this is speaking of the direct apprehension of reality, and when that happens, ego melts away, as does the distinction between our identity and that of the entire universe. We become one with the All.

To come directly into harmony with this reality, just simply say when doubts arise, "Not two." In this "not two," nothing is separate, nothing is excluded. No matter when or where, enlightenment means entering this truth. And this truth is beyond extension or diminution in time or space; in it, a single thought is ten thousand years.

Here, we again have the essence of the Zen perspective on reality. In this case, it is not abstract, but a concrete statement of how to avoid duality. The "not two" is like a mantra, from Hindu spiritual practice. Of course, as we go through our daily lives, our brains are constantly judging, discriminating, and doing all the things the sage has warned us to avoid. Simply resisting the brain's tendency in this direction is fruitless, but

Frank White

we can substitute a different thought for those discriminating thoughts.

So when you are in conflict with someone, instead of railing against their pig headedness, which really won't get you anywhere, "simply say 'not two.'" That two word phrase has the power to shift the context of the conflict dramatically.

Enlightenment, which we would all, of course, like to attain, is in fact realized just by getting this truth of "not-twoness." It seems so simple, yet it is so profound. Moreover, the sage tells us that this truth transcends time and space. He says that a single thought is 10,000 years when you are in that place, and I think he is implying that this one thought could be infinite.

Can we use "not-two" to reach this place? The only way to find out is to try it on a daily basis. I have been trying it out as a technique, and I can assert that it does work.

Emptiness here, emptiness there, but the infinite universe stands always before your eyes. Infinitely large and infinitely small; no difference, for definitions have vanished and no boundaries are seen. So, too, with being and non-being. Don't waste time in doubts and arguments that have nothing to do with this. One thing, all things, move among and intermingle without distinction. To live in this realization is to be without anxiety about non-perfection. To live in this faith is the road to non duality, because the non-dual is one with the trusting mind.

Emptiness is a major theme in Zen, and it is no accident that the patriarch ends his poem with a reference to it. He tells us that the infinite universe is always there, and that the difference between, say, an atom and a galaxy is no longer relevant. Although much of the academic endeavor is based on making these kinds of distinctions, the patriarch once again dismisses their value, once a person attains enlightenment.

The key to reaching an enlightened state is to avoid spending time uselessly arguing about issues like being and non-being. The patriarch also gives us a "pass" on trying to be perfect or make the world into something it is not. Non-duality and non-perfection go hand-in –hand, and can be tolerated with simple acceptance of things as they are. This reminds me of something the rector of my church, Jon Strand, often says in his sermons. He reminds us that what he calls "the perfection project" is doomed to failure. We are imperfect beings and trying to be something we are not isn't going to work.

Everything in this poem is really about non-duality, a realization that, while we continuously see duality, it is unity that represents the underlying reality. In other contexts, I have written about what astronauts see from orbit or the moon when they look at the Earth: they see unity, even though they know that there is great diversity there as well. This is what I call the Overview Effect, a cognitive shift that is, in a way, a direct apprehension of the unity and oneness of the Earth and the universe as a whole.[10]

Words! The Way is beyond language, for in it, there is no yesterday, no tomorrow, no today.

In this final, two-sentence conclusion, the Third Chinese Patriarch of Zen does a very Zen thing. Having used hundreds of words to explain his perspective, he concludes where he began: with the Way, and with the statement that it cannot be described with words, cannot be captured in language. And having let us know that enlightenment involves the transcending of space, he lets us know that the Way calls us to transcend time as well.

Frank White

Is this why, as he said at the very beginning, the Way is not difficult for those who have no preferences? Are words not the method by which we create preferences?

And now, I have used about 10,000 words to analyze what the Third Chinese Patriarch has told us in his poem. I don't know if it will be of value to you, the reader, but it has been incredibly valuable to me, and so I guess it has been a worthwhile exercise, even though it may not have moved me any closer to ultimate Truth! Thank you for taking this journey with me...

Postscript

When I began writing this essay, I did so with the same fascination that has influenced my spiritual life for many years: the question of how Buddhism and Christianity are related.

In fact, years ago, I somewhat jokingly said that I was establishing a new religion: "Tao Zen Christianity (TZC)." I announced that anyone could become a member, and that the basic tenets were these:

From Taoism, we get the Way;
From Zen, we get Enlightenment;
From Christianity, we get Salvation.

I had a couple of meetings with friends about starting this new religion, but it never went anywhere. My son Josh (jokingly) became the only adherent of TZC. Interestingly, Josh is now a Zen sensei, and pretty close to being a TZC person once again. I decided that I needed to be grounded in some tradition and returned to Christianity, eventually becoming active in a local Episcopalian church that is liberal enough to tolerate a larger perspective on Christ.

Still, I never lost my interest in Zen, and my spiritual practice evolved into reading a passage from *Hsin Hsin Ming* each day, along with a verse from the New Testament, always from the Gospels. I wanted the two sources of my spirituality to meet somewhere, to be congruent, and it was not until I decided to write this commentary that I saw a way for this to take place.

The key was to let go of traditional, orthodox Christian teachings and delve into the Gnostic tradition. Through the reading I have done while writing this commentary, I have come to see that early Christianity included a thread that was in fact very close to Buddhism in general and Zen in particular. This is the thread now known as "Gnosticism." However, we have to keep in mind that this was a name given to certain Christians by the orthodox church, which purged them from its membership.

"Gnosis" is Greek for knowledge, and one of the charges leveled against the so-called Gnostics was that they claimed to have secret knowledge that was unavailable to ordinary people. This is a debatable point, but it is true that this group of Christians showed more interest in having *knowledge* of Jesus than in holding certain *beliefs* about him. Again, Elaine Pagels captures this distinction in *Beyond Belief*.[11]

As she and others have pointed out, the Gnostic work, *Gospel of Thomas*, bears a strong resemblance to Buddhist teachings. There may simply be a similarity in the perspective of Jesus and that of Buddha, but it would be interesting if we found that Thomas did traveled to India after Jesus' death. This would establish a more direct connection between the two faiths.[12]

Pagels also documents the struggle between "orthodox" Christians, whose descendants created the Roman Catholic Church, and the so-called "Gnostics," who were suppressed by their fellow Christians. Their works were also banned and history more or less forgot them until a chance discovery of a treasure trove of Gnostic documents in 1945 at the village of Nag Hammadi.

The point is simply this: the gulf that *appears* to exist between Christianity and Buddhism is really a chasm between *orthodox* Christianity and Buddhism. For me, this is a great relief, and in the course of writing this commentary, I have come upon many examples of "Zen Christians" or "Christian Zen."

Here is the statement of one, called Zen Garland:

We follow Jesus as a Wisdom Teacher, whose emphasis on love and whose parables invite people to a radical expansion of consciousness, conscience, and community. Jesus used the expression, "Kingdom of heaven," to describe a "non dual consciousness" or " unitive consciousness," embodied through "an attitude of receptivity, a willingness to enter the flow, and a commitment to oneness." The hallmark of this awareness is that it sees no separation– not between God and humans, not between humans and other humans." (Cynthia Bourgeault)[13]

Doesn't this sound a lot like the perspective of Seng Ts'an, with its emphasis on unity and non-duality?

The critical point is this: Zen Garland's view of Jesus would not be congruent with orthodox Christianity, which would include almost every segment from Catholics to Evangelicals, but it would be quite consistent with the Gnostic perspective. Thus, whether Zen and Christianity can co-exist really depends on what one means by "Christianity." It is highly relevant that both Zen and Gnosticism are spiritual systems outside the mainstream of their own traditions, and this may be another reason that linking them seems somewhat straightforward.[14]

If we are able to see two of the great world religions as

Frank White

being similar and perhaps even seeking the same truths, I believe the Third Chinese Patriarch of Zen would be quietly pleased because "definitions have vanished and no boundaries are seen." Perhaps this is the path to social unity as well as personal peace and satisfaction. Or perhaps it is simply "the Great Way."

Notes

1. Elaine Pagels, *Beyond Belief: The Secret Gospel of Thomas*, Random House, New York, 2003.
2. Ibid.
3. Frank White, *The Overview Effect: Space Exploration and Human Evolution*, AIAA, Reston, VA, 2014.
4. *Gospel of Matthew*, 6:24, © Don Schwager, 2002
5. Pagels, op. cit.
6. Ibid.
7. *Gospel of Matthew*.
8. Rohit Sharma: Answer to a question online, https://www.quora.com
9. *Chinese Buddhist Encyclopedia*, quoting Michael Molloy, http://www.chinabuddhismencyclopedia.com/en/index.php/Tathatā.
10. White, op. cit
11. Pagels, op. cit.
12. Ibid.
13. Zen Garland community, http://zengarland.org
14. This link shows again how changing one's perspective can recontextualize a seemingly impossible problem.

Made in United States
Orlando, FL
20 June 2024